So you think you know Welsh rugby?

So you think you
know Welsh rugby?

Welsh Rugby
QUIZ

Matthew Jones

y Lolfa

Cover illustration: Sion Jones
Cover design: Y Lolfa

ISBN: 9781847710499

Printed on acid-free and partly recycled paper
and published and bound in Wales by
Y Lolfa Cyf., Talybont, Ceredigion SY24 5AP
e-mail ylolfa@ylolfa.com
website www.ylolfa.com
tel (01970) 832 304
fax 832 782

Introduction

Everyone in Wales thinks they know it all when it comes to the oval ball! This is a chance to see if you really do. Each round of this book can be considered as an individual quiz with the questions tending to get harder as you go from number one to ten. If you struggle to only get a couple correct then your knowledge is probably equivalent to that of a Scottish referee! If on the other hand you can get over seven correct then it's probably safe to say that you're a bit of a trivia guru.

Of course, if you manage to get ten out of ten then you are the equivalent of Carwyn James in the trivia world!!! Have fun…

Matthew Jones

Round 1

1. **The Brewery Field is home to which club side?**
   a) Bridgend
   b) Cross Keys
   c) Glamorgan Wanderers

2. **Who was the only uncapped player to be named in Warren Gatland's first Welsh squad, in preparation for the 2008 Six Nations tournament?**
   a) Jamie Roberts
   b) Robin Sowden-Taylor
   c) Lee Byrne

3. **During the 1984 Los Angeles Olympics, which Welsh winger reached the semi-finals of the 110 metre hurdles?**
   a) Steve Ford
   b) Nigel Walker
   c) David Manley

4. **Richmond signed Scott Quinnell from which rugby league side?**
   a) Bradford
   b) Wigan
   c) St Helen's

5. **Which second row was awarded the accolade of Pontypridd Player of the Year in 2001–02?**

   a) Ian Gough
   b) Robert Sidoli
   c) Brent Cockbain

6. **In New Zealand's 11-0 triumph over Llanelli in 1989, who scored their two tries?**

   a) Gary Whetton and Richard Loe
   b) Murray Pierce and Mike Brewer
   c) Andy Earl and Steve McDowell

7. **On the 14th of January 2006, Martyn Williams crossed which personal milestone?**

   a) Played his 50th game in the European cup, against Perpignan
   b) Made his 100th Arms Park appearance for the Cardiff Blues, against Munster
   c) Scored his 100th club try in all competitions, against Ulster

8. **What was so unusual about Aberavon's wins against Exeter and Guy's Hospital during the 1922–23 season?**

9. **During Wales' humiliating loss to Western Samoa in the 1992 Rugby World Cup, which Pontypool hooker had to replace Ritchie Collins in the back row?**

10. **What was the significance of Pontypridd's match against Ruthin on 14 March 1975?**

Round 2

1. **Ieuan Evans did not play for which of the following clubs?**
   a) Builth Wells
   b) Llanelli
   c) Bath

2. **Which English club signed Mefin Davies in December 2004?**
   a) London Irish
   b) Gloucester
   c) London Wasps

3. **Who was voted World Young Player of the Year in 2001?**
   a) Gavin Henson
   b) Dwayne Peel
   c) Michael Phillips

4. **Who became the first Welshman since Willie Llewellyn 92 years previously to score a hat-trick of tries on his debut in 1995?**
   a) Simon Hill
   b) Gareth Thomas
   c) Gareth Jones

5. **Leeds Rugby League Club paid a then world-record fee of £165,000 for a rugby union forward in 1990. Who did they buy?**

    a) Mark Jones
    b) Rowland Phillips
    c) David Young

6. **Dafydd James replaced which Llanelli centre in order to win his first cap against Australia in June 1996?**

    a) Neil Boobyer
    b) Nigel Davies
    c) Simon Davies

7. **Underhill Park is home to which club?**

    a) Pentyrch
    b) Tredegar
    c) Mumbles

8. **Scotland and Ireland both refused to play Wales in 1897. What was their reason?**

9. **Which village side beat Newport in the first round of the Welsh Cup during the 1980–81 season?**

10. **Who were the three players who started all six of Wales' games in the 1987 Rugby World Cup?**

Round 3

1. **Brent Cockbain is the younger brother of which former Australian forward?**
    - a) Dave
    - b) Jake
    - c) Matt

2. **In 1995, who became Wales' first professional full-time coach?**
    - a) Dennis John
    - b) Alan Lewis
    - c) Kevin Bowring

3. **'Growing up in Wales meant two things to me; rugby on Saturday and chapel on Sunday' was a quote attributed to which Welsh legend?**
    - a) Gareth Edwards
    - b) Barry John
    - c) Phil Bennet

4. **Former Cardiff forward Gregori Kacala represented which east European country?**
    - a) Slovakia
    - b) Romania
    - c) Poland

5. **Who made his first appearance for Pontypridd against South Wales Police on the 14th of April 1990?**
    - a) Steele Lewis
    - b) Paul John
    - c) Neil Jenkins

6. **Which dual code international made his union debut for Wales in the 1987 World Cup third place play off against Australia in Rotorua?**

   a) Richard Webster
   b) Jonathan Griffiths
   c) Mark Jones

7. **In 1935, who became the first-ever club side to defeat New Zealand?**

   a) Newport
   b) Cardiff
   c) Swansea

8. **Which scrum half won three Lions caps on the 1977 tour of New Zealand before making his Wales debut against Australia in 1978?**

9. **Who was Llanelli's top try scorer for eight consecutive seasons between 1951–52 and 1958–59?**

10. **Who were the three singers that performed the Welsh national anthem during Wales' famous win against England in their 2005 Grand Slam winning season?**

Round 4

1. **Who made his 101st and final appearance for Australia, in their 28-19 defeat of Wales on the 1st of December 1996?**
   a) David Campese
   b) Nick Farr-Jones
   c) Rod McCall

2. **The Welsh Young Player of the Year award for 2005–06 was given to which Ospreys player?**
   a) Ian Evans
   b) James Hook
   c) Alun Wyn Jones

3. **Which Stradey Park hooker made 55 appearances in the European cup?**
   a) Andrew Lamerton
   b) David Fox
   c) Robin McBryde

4. **Who was the only Welshman to have played in the 1987 and 1999 Rugby World Cups?**
   a) Ieuan Evans
   b) Gareth Llewellyn
   c) David Young

5. **What is Charlie Faulkner's real fist name?**
   a) Beverley
   b) Aubrey
   c) Cuthbert

6. **Who scored Wales' only try in their 18-13 win over Australia in 1981?**

    a) Gareth Davies

    b) Richard Moriaty

    c) Gwyn Evans

7. **Jack Hurrell and Leighton Jenkins scored a try apiece for the Black and Ambers against which international team on the 23rd of November 1957?**

    a) Fiji

    b) South Africa

    c) Australia

8. **Dave Tiueti created history on the 5th of September 2003 when he scored a try at the Gnoll. What was the significance of this try?**

9. **Who was the first Welshman to play at number 8, wearing the number 8 shirt?**

10. **Who scored a try against England on his test debut in 1959, and in his final international, coincidentally, against the same opposition in 1967?**

Round 5

1. **On the 15th of March 1997, who scored the last international try at the National Stadium, Cardiff Arms Park?**
   a) Robert Howley
   b) Phil de Glanville
   c) Mike Catt

2. **Thames, New Zealand was the birthplace of which centre?**
   a) Tom Shanklin
   b) Sonny Parker
   c) Mark Taylor

3. **Mike Ruddock was Director of Coaching at which Irish province between 1997 and 2000?**
   a) Munster
   b) Leinster
   c) Ulster

4. **What was unusual about the drop goal executed by Willy Davies against Ireland on March 11th 1939?**
   a) First 3 point drop goal scored by a Welshman
   b) Last 2 point drop goal scored in Cardiff
   c) Last 4 point drop goal scored by Wales

5. **Which club provided the largest number of players for the 1971 Lions tour of Australia and New Zealand?**

    a) Cardiff

    b) London Welsh

    c) Llanelli

6. **St Peter's RFC is known by which nickname?**

    a) The rocks

    b) The green birds

    c) The daffodils

7. **Maesteg maintained their Welsh premiership status at the end of the 2005–06 season with a play off win against which side?**

    a) Beddau

    b) Whitland

    c) Bonymaen

8. **Name the Welsh centre who scored ten tries and a total of 59 points on the 1903 Lions tour of South Africa.**

9. **Who scored seven tries in nine appearances in a Welsh Rugby Union jersey before moving from Cardiff to Salford in 1969?**

10. **Pontypool were only able to score a single try against Swansea in their 1983 Welsh Cup Final win. Who scored the try?**

Round 6

1. Who captained the 1977 Lions tour of New Zealand?

    a) Graham Price

    b) Phil Bennett

    c) Steve Fenwick

2. How many scrums, against the head, did Wales lose during their whole 2005 Grand Slam winning Six Nations campaign?

    a) 0

    b) 1

    c) 3

3. Three players captained Wales in their humiliating 96–13 loss to South Africa at the Loftus Versfeld in 1998. Who were they?

    a) Mike Griffiths, Colin Charvis and Steve Williams

    b) Mark Taylor, John Davies and Andy Moore

    c) Kingsley Jones, Paul John and Garin Jenkins

4. Which Welsh flyer scored a brace of tries in Wales' 30-15 victory over Scotland in February 2008?

    a) Shane Williams

    b) Mark Jones

    c) Lee Byrne

5. **Against Romania in 2001, who became the first Welsh forward to score a hat-trick of tries?**

    a) Geraint P Lewis
    b) Colin Charvis
    c) Scott Quinnell

6. **Who had the final touch of the ball when Wales claimed their 2005 Grand Slam triumph against Ireland?**

    a) Stephen Jones
    b) Dwayne Peel
    c) Martyn Williams

7. **Which club is known as the 'old firm'?**

    a) Nantymoel
    b) Mountain Ash
    c) Pontypool United

8. **Graham Price played in all four Lions tests of the 1983 tour of New Zealand. Which two other Welsh props gained caps on the tour?**

9. **London Welsh lost their only ever English Cup Final in 1985. Who was the opposition?**

10. **Newport legend Arthur Gould was the cause of Wales being temporarily banned from international matches. What was the reason?**

Round 7

1. **Who scored the famous winning try in Wales' 32-31 victory over England at Wembley in 1999?**
   - a) Ben Evans
   - b) Nick Walne
   - c) Scott Gibbs

2. **In 1957, Llanelli became the first British team to play in which vodka-loving country?**
   - a) Yugoslavia
   - b) Russia
   - c) Romania

3. **How many tries did Ieuan Evans score against Canada in the 1987 Rugby World Cup?**
   - a) 4
   - b) 5
   - c) 6

4. **Andrew Hore played what role during Wales's Grand Slam year of 2005?**
   - a) Defence coach
   - b) Strength and conditioning coach
   - c) Statistical analyst

5. **Why were Ken Jones and Jack Kyle omitted from the 1955 Lions tour to South Africa?**
   - a) They played their club rugby in France
   - b) The Lions had a policy of choosing only players under 30 years of age
   - c) They did not have passports

6. **Who did Wales beat to record their first international win in January 1882?**

      a) England

      b) Cornwall

      c) Ireland

7. **Which New Zealand second row scored his only ever test try, in 1988 against Wales?**

      a) Murray Pierce

      b) Gary Whetton

      c) Ian Jones

8. **Former Newport prop Adrian Garvey played international rugby for which two countries?**

9. **In Wales' second tour match against Japan in 2001, there were three sons of former Welsh internationals in action. Who were they?**

10. **A seat reserved for an important public figure at the old National stadium, Cardiff Arms Park fetched £1,600.00 when sold at auction. Who was this person?**

Round 8

1. **In 2002, who became the first Welsh side to reach the European shield final?**
   - a) Swansea
   - b) Pontypridd
   - c) Bridgend

2. **Who captained Wales to an embarrassing 63-6 loss to Australia at Ballymore in 1991?**
   - a) Ieuan Evans
   - b) Kevin Phillips
   - c) Paul Thorburn

3. **Who scored the only try of the game to give Wales a famous 3-0 win against the All Blacks at Cardiff Arms Park in December 1905?**
   - a) Gwyn Nicholls
   - b) Cliff Pritchard
   - c) Teddy Morgan

4. **Aberavon have only recorded a single win in European competition. Who was it against?**
   - a) Bristol
   - b) Spain
   - c) Pau

5. **The first Welshman to tour New Zealand and Australia with a representative team was W. H. Thomas in 1888. Which team did he play for?**

   a) Barbarians

   b) The British Army

   c) Cambridge University

6. **Name the former Welsh international who became the International Rugby Board secretary in 1988.**

   a) Keith Rowlands

   b) Kelvin Coslett

   c) Alun Pask

7. **What feat was achieved by Hayden Tanner, Wilf Wooler and Norman Biggs?**

   a) Played for Wales before and after World War Two

   b) Played for Wales while still in school

   c) Broke an arm during an international match, but carried on playing until the end of the game

8. **Which tactic was banned in the 1968–69 season, which will always be associated with Clive Rowlands?**

9. **Scott Gibbs earned himself which unwanted accolade against the Dragons on 12th of September 2003?**

10. **Which flanker made his Wales debut at the age of 33, on Wales' 2004 summer tour to Argentina and South Africa?**

Round 9

1. **At 6 feet 10 inches, who became Wales' tallest ever player in 1994?**

   a) Anthony Copsey

   b) Derwyn Jones

   c) Steve Williams

2. **An entire club front row represented Wales for the first time against France in 1975. Name the club.**

   a) Ebbw Vale

   b) Abertillery

   c) Pontypool

3. **Jeff Squire won the Welsh cup on two occasions. Which two clubs did he win them with?**

   a) Bridgend and Swansea

   b) Newport and Pontypool

   c) Llanelli and Neath

4. **Dunvant lost by a single point to which touring nation on the 2nd of October 1993?**

   a) Tonga

   b) Japan

   c) Namibia

5. **Trevor Lloyd became which club's first Lion in 1955?**

   a) Devonport services

   b) Maesteg

   c) Newbridge

6. **Who was the 1992 Welsh player of the year?**

    a) Emyr Lewis
    b) Stuart Davies
    c) Richard Webster

7. **The first-ever four point try by a Welshman was scored against England at Twickenham in 1972. Who was the try scorer?**

    a) Roy Bergiers
    b) John Bevan
    c) J. P. R Williams

8. **Which former Newport full back won 8 caps for Australia before earning another 12 for Italy?**

9. **Welsh winger Ken Jones represented Great Britain in the Olympic games. Name the event in which he won a silver medal, the year, and the host city for the games.**

10. **What is the connection between Clive Rowlands, John R. Evans and James Bevan?**

Round 10

1. **Which prop was voted 2005–06 Welsh player of the year?**
   - a) Gethin Jenkins
   - b) Duncan Jones
   - c) Adam Jones

2. **During the 1999 Rugby World Cup Neil Jenkins became the world's highest points scorer, but whose record did he beat?**
   - a) Grant Fox
   - b) Gavin Hastings
   - c) Michael Lynagh

3. **Against Ireland in 2003, who became the 28th pair of brothers to play together for Wales?**
   - a) Garan and Deiniol Evans
   - b) Aled and Nathan Brew
   - c) Jamie and Nicky Robinson

4. **Which club lost to Llanelli in both the 1974 and 1975 Welsh Cup Finals?**
   - a) Swansea
   - b) Neath
   - c) Aberavon

5. **During Wales' dire 9-0 victory against Ireland at Cardiff Arms Park in 1961, which fly half scored all of the home side's points?**

   a) Ken Richards
   b) Alan Rees
   c) David Watkins

6. **Which of the following did not play in all four Lions tests on the 1977 tour of New Zealand?**

   a) Steve Fenwick
   b) Graham Price
   c) Gareth Evans

7. **In 1926 Wales drew with England 3-3. Six members of the Welsh pack were members of the same profession. What was their occupation?**

   a) Policemen
   b) Teachers
   c) Solicitors

8. **The *Glasgow Sunday Herald* caused an international storm by printing which article in the year 2000?**

9. **Name the three Widnes players in the Welsh Rugby League side that beat Papua New Guinea 68-0 in 1991.**

10. **At the start of the 1971 Lions tour to Australia and New Zealand, which side was John Bevan registered to play for?**

Round 11

1. **For which Gwent club did Brian Price ply his trade?**

    a) Pontypool

    b) Newport

    c) Ebbw Vale

2. **Which Welsh hooker was selected for the 1997 Lions tour of South Africa?**

    a) Barry Williams

    b) Nigel Meek

    c) Andrew Lamerton

3. **Who famously scored a touchline conversion with only two minutes left on the clock to beat Scotland 19-18 in 1971?**

    a) Barry John

    b) John Taylor

    c) J. P. R. Williams

4. **How many games did the Celtic Warriors play in the European Cup?**

    a) 6

    b) 7

    c) 12

5. **Which New Zealander scored four of his side's record ten tries against Wales at Lancaster Park on the 28th of May 1988?**

    a) John Gallagher

    b) Terry Wright

    c) John Kirwan

6. **Glan-yr-afon park is the home of which club?**
   a) Blackwood
   b) Cross Keys
   c) Cardigan

7. **In 1985, London Welsh lost their only ever English Cup Final. Who was the opposition?**
   a) Leicester
   b) Gloucester
   c) Bath

8. **Who was the Oxford University, London Welsh and Bridgend full back who played for Wales between 1933 and 1939, before becoming one of the world's leading rugby journalists?**

9. **Carwyn James was once a teacher at which famous public school?**

10. **On the 1971 Lions tour, an all-Welsh back row played together in the third test at Wellington. Name all three players.**

Round 12

1. **St Helen's is home to which club side?**
   - a) Swansea
   - b) Bridgend
   - c) Cardiff

2. **Gareth and Glyn Llewellyn played together for Wales and which club side in the early 1990's?**
   - a) Pontypridd
   - b) Glamorgan Wanderers
   - c) Neath

3. **Gareth Edwards never won a Welsh Cup Final, but how many times did he appear for the losing side?**
   - a) 2
   - b) 3
   - c) 5

4. **Who became Wales' 1000th capped player when he made his international debut against South Africa in June 2002?**
   - a) Mefin Davies
   - b) Jonathan Thomas
   - c) Michael Owen

5. **How many Llanelli Scarlets players started a Six Nations match in the 2005 season?**
   - a) 4
   - b) 5
   - c) 6

6. **South Wales Police provided which player for Wales' 1991 Rugby world Cup squad?**
    a) Kevin Moseley
    b) Ritchie Collins
    c) Hugh Williams-Jones

7. **Who scored a 45 yard penalty goal that gave Wales a 3-3 draw against England at Twickenham in 1958?**
    a) Terry Davies
    b) Cliff Morgan
    c) Lloyd Williams

8. **Name the Newport player that toured with the Lions in 1930, joined Wigan in 1932, then played for Great Britain down under in 1936.**

9. **Andrew Gibbs was the only player to represent Wales in the 1995 Five Nations from which Gwent club?**

10. **Gwyn Nicholls achieved something in 1899, which was repeated by Reg Skrimshire in 1903. Cliff Morgan also did it in 1955 as well as Ken Jones in 1962. What was it?**

Round 13

1. **Between 1987 and 1998, who scored a then record 33 tries in 72 appearances for Wales?**
    a) Ieuan Evans
    b) Arthur Emyr
    c) Wayne Proctor

2. **Who scored the first-ever try at the Millennium Stadium?**
    a) Mark Taylor
    b) Gareth Thomas
    c) Scott Gibbs

3. **What were Swansea's first-ever shirt colours?**
    a) Red and white vertical stripes
    b) Green and white quarters
    c) Blue and white horizontal stripes

4. **With 29 caps to his name, who held the record as most capped Welsh outside half for nearly 40 years, after making his international debut in 1951?**
    a) Carwyn James
    b) Cliff Morgan
    c) Cliff Ashton

5. **Which of the following nicknames has not been associated with Caerphilly RFC?**
    a) The Jackdaws
    b) The Cheesemen
    c) The Trawlers

6. **Who scored a try on his 50th Welsh appearance in the 47–8 defeat of Italy in 2008?**

   a) Tom Shanklin

   b) Shane Williams

   c) Stephen Jones

7. **Haldane Luscombe was born in which South African city?**

   a) Johannesburg

   b) Cape Town

   c) Pretoria

8. **Who took over from Gwyn Jones as Wales' 111th skipper?**

9. **Between 1961 and 1985, who made a record 877 appearances for Pontypridd?**

10. **The British rugby tour of Australia in 1899 was the first to include international players from each of the four home countries. A Cardiff player scored in the first test and finished the tour as the top try scorer. Name him.**

Round 14

1. **How many games did Wales win under caretaker coach Scott Johnson?**

    a) 0

    b) 1

    c) 2

2. **Who successfully kicked 24 conversions in only four internationals against Wales between 1987 and 1989?**

    a) Hugo Porta

    b) Didier Camberabero

    c) Grant Fox

3. **The 1998 Welsh Cup final between Llanelli and Ebbw Vale was held at which football ground?**

    a) Ashton Gate, Bristol

    b) Villa Park, Birmingham

    c) Ninian Park, Cardiff

4. **Who became the 150th player to win senior international honours from Llanelli in 1995?**

    a) Spencer John

    b) Craig Quinnell

    c) Justin Thomas

5. **Who was Wales' first post-World War II outside half?**

    a) Bleddyn Williams

    b) Jack Matthews

    c) Billy Cleaver

6. **Neath's first captain Dr T. P. Whittington was capped by which country?**

   a) England
   b) Ireland
   c) Scotland

7. **Charles Prydderch Lewis of Llandovery became the first Welshman to do what?**

   a) Throw a ball into a lineout
   b) Play on his own, as a full back
   c) Wear shorts that were above the knee

8. **Which former Newbridge Hooker played 25 rugby league tests for Great Britain between 1954 and 1960?**

9. **Who connects Maesteg with both the Gauteng Falcons and London Irish?**

10. **The Newfoundland dogs was the first club for which former Rodney Parade favourite?**

Round 15

1. **During the late 1970s and early 1980s, which legendary prop played 39 successive internationals?**

    a) Clive Williams

    b) Charlie Faulkner

    c) Graham Price

2. **Colin Charvis joined which French second division side following the 2003 World Cup?**

    a) Narbonne

    b) Montpellier

    c) Tarbes

3. **In 1969 Phil Bennett made his international debut in Paris. What was unusual about this appearance?**

    a) Youngest ever international

    b) First-ever Welsh international substitute

    c) He played at Hooker

4. **Bedford Blues appointed which former full back as Director of rugby in 2005?**

    a) Mike Rayer

    b) Anthony Clement

    c) Paul Thorburn

5. **Against which club did the Ospreys gain their first-ever Celtic League away-win in the Principality?**

    a) Llanelli Scarlets

    b) Celtic Warriors

    c) Cardiff Blues

CARDIFF
CAERDYDD

6. **Wales became the first country to alter their formation in which way against Scotland in 1886?**

   a) Played 10 forwards
   b) Used 4 threequaters
   c) Fielded 2 scrum halves

7. **Jack Bassett captained Wales on nine occasions in the early 1930s. Which club did he play for?**

   a) Penarth
   b) Torquay
   c) Birkenhead Park

8. **Who did Warren Gatland name as Welsh captain for his first game in charge against England in February 2008?**

9. **Who became the 19th set of brothers to play together for Scotland, when they lined up against the Welsh in 2005?**

10. **Which toe-punting second row kicked points for Wales in their 1975 and 1976 Five Nations Championship winning seasons?**

Round 16

1. **Which Pontypridd legend is known as 'The Chief', due to his resemblance of the Chief Bronden character in *One Flew over the Cuckoo's Nest*?**

     a) Dale McIntosh

     b) Jason Lewis

     c) Phill John

2. **During Wales' 17-15 win against Ireland at Lansdowne Road in 1994, which Irish stand-off missed a penalty with eight minutes left on the clock?**

     a) David Humphreys

     b) Eric Elwood

     c) Ronan O'Gara

3. **Which prop moved from Leicester Tigers to Worcester Warriors in the summer of 2006?**

     a) Chris Horseman

     b) Ben Evans

     c) Darren Morris

4. **Who scored a hat-trick of tries for Cardiff against Newport in the 1986 Welsh Cup Final?**

     a) Adrian Hadley

     b) Mark Ring

     c) Terry Holmes

5. **Iestyn Harris scored two tries to ensure a 24-22 Welsh win at Stradey Park in the 2000 Rugby League World Cup. Which Middle East country was the opposition?**

   a) Jordan
   b) Lebanon
   c) Saudi Arabia

6. **Former Swansea coach John Plumtree won South Africa's Currie cup four times in the 1990s. Who did he play for?**

   a) Northern Transvaal
   b) Natal Sharks
   c) Western Province

7. **The Welsh Grand Slam of 1950 was the first since when?**

   a) 1911
   b) 1921
   c) 1931

8. **The Welsh Sportsman of the Year award was presented to which hooker on his retirement in 1962?**

9. **Allan Bateman played for which Australian Rugby League side?**

10. **Who became the first Llanelli player to tour with the British and Irish Lions in 1930?**

Round 17

1. **Wayne Proctor scored 11 tries in 39 internationals. What was his recognised position?**
   - a) Centre
   - b) Wing
   - c) Flanker

2. **In 2006, who became the first player to score 25 Heineken European Cup tries?**
   - a) Dafydd James
   - b) Gareth Thomas
   - c) Kevin Morgan

3. **David Evans was the only player from which club in Wales' 1995 Rugby World Cup squad?**
   - a) Bridgend
   - b) Treorchy
   - c) Newbridge

4. **Hooker Ben Daly joined Newport Gwent Dragons in 2006 from which club side?**
   - a) Worcester Warriors
   - b) Bayonne
   - c) Viadana

5. **Robert Norster was banned from international rugby in 1986 for a retaliatory punch on which fellow second row?**
   - a) Richard Moriaty
   - b) Phil May
   - c) Steve Sutton

6. **Maesteg's Gwyn Evans broke two records during Wales' 22-12 win over France in February 1982. The first was reaching 50 international points in the fastest time for a Welshman, requiring only six matches to do so. What was the second?**

    a) First player to kick six penalty goals in a Five Nations match

    b) First full back to score a hat-trick of tries against France

    c) The only person to kick three drop goals in a Five Nations game

7. **Ireland's match with Wales in 1962 was postponed from March to November. Why?**

    a) Wales wouldn't travel due to IRA activity in mainland Britain

    b) Smallpox outbreak in South Wales

    c) Lansdowne Road had to be re-surfaced due to a mole infestation

8. **Who said the infamous phrase 'Get your retaliation in first' during the 1971 Lions tour?**

9. **A £90,000 transfer from Warrington to Cardiff saw which player become the first to move back from rugby league to rugby union in 1995?**

10. **Tim Fauval will be remembered historically for which event in 1988?**

Round 18

1. Which club side plays at Rodney Parade?

    a) Newport

    b) Cross Keys

    c) Brynmawr

2. Which Llanelli forward kicked a controversial drop goal against Neath in the 1993 Welsh Cup Final?

    a) Mark Perego

    b) Lyn Jones

    c) Emyr Lewis

3. In 1967, who became Wales' first rugby coach?

    a) David Nash

    b) Clive Rowlands

    c) John Dawes

4. Which second row, won international recognition at volleyball and fishing as a youngster?

    a) Chris Wyatt

    b) Deiniol Jones

    c) Alun Wyn Jones

5. Non Evans became the third woman to win 50 caps in Wales' 30-10 loss to Scotland in 2004. Which English club was she registered with?

    a) Saracens

    b) Wasps

    c) Clifton

6. **Japanese manager Shigeru Konno saw his team lose 62-14 at Cardiff Arms Park in an uncapped international back in 1973. What had he previously been trained as?**

   a) Origami designer
   b) World War II kamikaze pilot
   c) Whale hunter

7. **Wales won the 2007 Hong Kong sevens plate by beating Argentina 26-19 in the final. Who scored the winning try in a thrilling climax to the game?**

   a) Wayne Evans
   b) Lee Beach
   c) Tal Selley

8. **Which legendary centre scored a club record 41 tries for Cardiff in their 1947-48 season?**

9. **What was unusual about Ireland's line-up against Wales on 12th April 1884?**

10. **Name Wales' two try scorers in their dramatic 19-26 victory over England at Twickenham in 2008.**

Round 19

1. **Who skipped past five tacklers to score a famous try in Wales' 25-20 win over Scotland in 1988?**
   a) Carwyn Davies
   b) Adrian Hadley
   c) Ieuan Evans

2. **Who captained Wales to their 1976 Grand Slam?**
   a) Gareth Edwards
   b) Graham Price
   c) Mervyn Davies

3. **Television presenter Sarra Elgan is married to which Llanelli Scarlets player?**
   a) Stephen Jones
   b) Simon Easterby
   c) Dafydd Jones

4. **Dai Young is the only man to have done what with the British Lions?**
   a) Toured with the Lions in three different decades
   b) The only Welsh forward to have scored a hat-trick of tries in a Lions game
   c) The only player to have been sent off in three separate tours

5. **Ioan Bebb's rugby career was ended when he suffered a detached retina following a punch by an international second row. Who was the other player involved?**
   a) Chris Stephens
   b) Adam Jones
   c) Mike Voyle

6. **Rob Andrew scored all of England's points in their 21-18 win over the Welsh at Twickenham in 1986. Who did he play for at the time?**
   a) Coventry
   b) Nottingham
   c) Headingley

7. **Ken Jones' 43rd cap against France in 1956 broke the British Isles record for *most capped international*. Which Irishman previously held the record?**
   a) George Stephenson
   b) Fred Moran
   c) Paul Murray

8. **Who made a try scoring debut in Wales' 16-15 win over Ireland in 1992?**

9. **Reverend Rowland Williams introduced rugby to the Welsh nation in 1850 via which educational institution?**

10. **The 1973 New Zealand team which beat Newport 15-20 at Rodney Parade were captained by which Kiwi legend?**

Round 20

1. **Toulouse's Trevor Brennan received a life ban in 2007 for assaulting an Ulster fan. Who was the Welsh player involved?**
   a) Gareth Thomas
   b) Martyn Williams
   c) James Hook

2. **Denzil Williams played club rugby for which Gwent side?**
   a) Abertillery
   b) Ebbw Vale
   c) Newport

3. **Who won Wales' Strongest Man competition in 1992?**
   a) Mike Griffiths
   b) Richard Webster
   c) Robin McBryde

4. **Secom in Japan was the previous club of which international player who joined Llanelli Scarlets in the summer of 2005?**
   a) Inoke Afeaki
   b) Regan King
   c) Francois 'Hottie' Louw

5. **Australia played Western Samoa in the 1991 rugby World Cup at which Welsh ground?**
   a) Stradey Park
   b) St Helen's
   c) Pontypool Park

6. **Who captained Wales to an 11-6 victory over England at Twickenham in 1966?**

   a) Clive Rowlands
   b) Alun Pask
   c) Norman Gale

7. **Newport full back Garfield Owen failed to make his international debut against England in 1955 due to what injury?**

   a) Broken toe, caused by dropping a pint of milk on his foot
   b) Twisted back, while eating a bacon sandwich in bed
   c) Gashed knee, due to falling on snow covered brambles

8. **Charlie Thomas and Alf Morgan introduced rugby to which Neath valley village while installing boilers at Glyncastle Colliery?**

9. **Who in the 1980's became the only Aberavon player to captain Wales?**

10. **Which 17-times-capped England international captained Newport in their 15-16 win over Cardiff in the 1977 Welsh Cup final?**

Round 21

1. **Gavin Quinnell left the Llanelli Scarlets in the summer of 2006 to join which English side?**
   a) Worcester Warriors
   b) London Irish
   c) Sale Sharks

2. **J. P. R. Williams faced England on eleven occasions. How many times did he end up on the losing side?**
   a) 0
   b) 1
   c) 11

3. **Fiji wing Rupeni Caucaunibuca was unable to play for the Pacific Islands against Wales in 2006. What was the reason?**
   a) He was in jail
   b) He had lost his passport
   c) He'd turned up in Rome, thinking he was playing against Italy

4. **Who captained Wales in their 500th international against Japan in 2001?**
   a) Robert Howley
   b) Andrew Moore
   c) Geraint Lewis

5. **The International Rugby Board was founded in 1886 at a meeting in Manchester. This agreement was between Wales and two other countries. Who were the other countries?**

    a) Scotland and Ireland

    b) England and France

    c) New Zealand and Australia

6. **John and Bill Roberts were brothers that played together at club level, and in 1929, also at international level. This was when they were both selected to play against England. Which club did they represent?**

    a) Abertillery

    b) Bridgend

    c) Cardiff

7. **Swansea's first-ever European match was a 17-13 loss to Munster at Thomond Park on the 1st of November 1995. Who was Swansea's only try scorer, and hence, the club's first-ever try scorer in the European Cup?**

    a) Alan Harris

    b) Mark Taylor

    c) Aled Williams

8. **Who was the first Welshman to captain a Lions tour?**

9. **Who was Wales' only-ever present second row in their three 1991 Rugby World Cup games?**

10. **John Gwilliam captained Wales to both 1950 and 1952 Grand Slams. Which club did he represent at the time?**

Round 22

1. **Who are known as the Welsh 'All Blacks'?**
   a) Carmarthen Quins
   b) Whitland
   c) Neath

2. **Chippenham magistrates gave a one-month driving ban to which Ospreys player in 2006 after he was caught driving at 110mph on the M4?**
   a) Alun Wyn Jones
   b) Gavin Henson
   c) Barry Williams

3. **Which Welsh centre won the European Cup with Northampton in 2000?**
   a) Allan Bateman
   b) Neil Boobyer
   c) Scott Gibbs

4. **Who is Swansea's post-war all-time top try scorer?**
   a) Roger Blyth
   b) Tony Swift
   c) Arthur Emyr

5. **In Wales' 15-9 loss to Romania in 1988, all four three-quarters were provided by the same club. Which club was it?**
   a) Cardiff
   b) Llanelli
   c) Bridgend

6. **In Wales' draw with South Africa in 1970, who contributed all six of his team's points with a try and a penalty kick?**

      a) Barry John

      b) Gareth Edwards

      c) Phil Bennett

7. **Who scored both tries in Wales' 6-3 win over France at Paris in 1953?**

      a) Terry Davies

      b) Rees Stephens

      c) Gareth Griffiths

8. **During Wales' 2005 Grand Slam winning campaign, who was the only back to have sat on the bench for all five matches?**

9. **Who was the 31 year old Llanelli player that made his debut in Wales' 11-3 win over England at Twickenham in 1988?**

10. **Who scored 228 points in 14 matches during his first season for Cardiff in 1999-2000?**

Round 23

1. **How many Welsh rugby union caps did Pontypool's David Bishop gain before moving to Rugby League?**

    a) 0

    b) 1

    c) 50

2. **Which French side beat Cardiff in the inaugural European Cup final at the National Stadium, Cardiff Arms Park in the 1995-96 season?**

    a) Brive

    b) Montferrand

    c) Toulouse

3. **Speaking in Welsh during a post-match dinner in 1986, Jonathan Davies described the opposition as 'the dirtiest team I have ever played against'. The opposition unknowingly applauded, but who were they?**

    a) New Zealand

    b) Fiji

    c) Tonga

4. **Against Romania in 2004, who became the seventh Welshman to score four tries in a match?**

    a) Tom Shanklin

    b) Colin Charvis

    c) Shane Williams

5. **Mark Ring became coach of which Limerick-based club in 2006?**

      a) Old Crescent

      b) St Joseph's

      c) Dungannon

6. **Bill Beaumont captained England to a 9-8 win over Wales at Twickenham in February 1980. Which club did he play for at the time?**

      a) Broughton Park

      b) Fylde

      c) Harrogate

7. **Who scored both tries in Wales' 8-3 win over Scotland in 1966?**

      a) Stuart Watkins

      b) Lyn Davies

      c) Ken Jones

8. **Who was the 33-times-capped South African centre who joined Cardiff in the summer of 2000?**

9. **Who helped Overmarch Parma beat Newport Gwent Dragons in the 2006 European Cup play off, then ironically scored the winning try for the Dragons against Calvisano in the following year's play off?**

10. **During Wales' 19-0 loss to New Zealand at Lancaster Park, Christchurch, in 1969, who became the first Welsh forward to earn a cap as a replacement?**

Round 24

1. **Which Welsh club reached the 2003 European Shield final?**

     a) Dunvant

     b) Glamorgan Wanderers

     c) Caerphilly

2. **How many Celtic League titles did the Llanelli Scarlets win under Gareth Jenkins?**

     a) 0

     b) 1

     c) 5

3. **Which former Welsh Schools international made his England debut, against Australia, in November 1984?**

     a) Stuart Barnes

     b) Les Cusworth

     c) John Carleton

4. *My life in International Rugby* **was an autobiography published in 2001, where the author admitted taking amphetamines before Wales' 1986 win against Scotland. Who wrote the book?**

     a) Phil Lewis

     b) Robert Jones

     c) Adrian Hadley

5. **Who played his 92nd and final International against Wales at Wembley on 29th November 1997?**

   a) Michael Lynagh
   b) Sean Fitzpatrick
   c) Jeremy Guscott

6. **Wales beat Scotland 8-0 in February 1960. One club supplied the whole of the back row. Which club?**

   a) Newport
   b) Pontypool
   c) Swansea

7. **What was the significance of Wales' match against Scotland in 1974?**

   a) 100th capped International at the Arms Park
   b) First International match to be played on a Sunday
   c) The only ever Five Nations match to have been refereed by a Canadian

8. **Who kicked four drop goals in Cardiff's 12-9 win over Llanelli in November 1970?**

9. **Which World Cup final referee played for Neath?**

10. **Name the Newport and London Welsh three-quarter who comes first in the alphabetic listings of Welsh Internationals.**

Round 25

1. **Who won the 2006-07 Welsh Premiership for the third consecutive time?**

   a) Neath

   b) Ebbw Vale

   c) Pontypridd

2. **Which Welsh prop made his 50th appearance for his country in Wales' 20-32 defeat to Australia in the 2007 Rugby World Cup?**

   a) Duncan Jones

   b) Adam Jones

   c) Gethin Jenkins

3. **In which year did Wales suffer their first-ever Five Nations whitewash, losing all four matches?**

   a) 1989

   b) 1990

   c) 1992

4. **Who captained Swansea to the 1997–98 Welsh League Championship?**

   a) Rob Appleyard

   b) Mark Taylor

   c) Garin Jenkins

5. **Who scored 47 tries in 51 appearances for Cardiff between 1947 and 1949?**

   a) Maldwyn James

   b) Frank Trott

   c) Les Williams

6. **Wales' 19–26 defeat of England in 2008 was their first win at Twickhenham for how many years?**

     a) 20

     b) 22

     c) 24

7. **Which Scottish forward kicked a magnificent drop goal from near the touchline, in Scotlands shock 19-0 win over Wales in 1951?**

     a) Hamish Inglis

     b) Hamish Dawson

     c) Peter Kininmonth

8. **In 1997, which Llanelli forward received a two year ban for using anabolic steroids?**

9. **Why is Sunday 6th of October 1991 such a significant – if not depressing – date in the history of Welsh rugby?**

10. **Steve Ford had a lifetime ban from playing rugby union lifted in 1988. The cause of the ban was playing in a trial match for a rugby league side. Which club was it?**

Round 26

1. **Who captained the 1971 British and Irish Lions to Australia and New Zealand?**

    a) Gareth Edwards

    b) John Taylor

    c) John Dawes

2. **Who became the first Englishman in nine years to score four tries in a game, during Wales' humiliating 62-5 loss in their 2007 Rugby World Cup warm up match at Twickenham?**

    a) Nick Easter

    b) Shaun Perry

    c) Jason Robinson

3. **Which New Zealand forward scored a drop goal in the All Blacks' 42-7 win over Wales at Wembley in 1997?**

    a) Josh Kronfeld

    b) Zinzan Brooke

    c) Taine Randell

4. **Which of the following clubs was not represented by a player in the Welsh team that beat New Zealand 3-0 in 1905?**

    a) Llanelli

    b) Pill Harriers

    c) Penygraig

5. **Who left Cardiff for a period in the 1954-55 season to join Bective Rangers in Dublin?**

   a) Haydn Morris
   b) Cliff Morgan
   c) Alun Thomas

6. **Prop David Maddocks left Newport Gwent Dragons in the summer of 2007. Which English side did he join?**

   a) Leeds
   b) Northampton
   c) Coventry

7. **Name the Swansea forward who was his club's top points scorer for five consecutive seasons between 1925 and 1930.**

   a) Dick Huxtable
   b) Howell John
   c) Dai Parker

8. **Who was the first New Zealand-born player to represent Wales?**

9. **Who became Neath's first double Lion, following his selection for both the 1977 and 1980 tours?**

10. **Aberavon were only told of their promotion to the top tier of Welsh rugby four days before the start of the 1998–99 season. Why?**

Round 27

1. **Sardis Road is home to which club side?**

   a) Bedwas

   b) Carmarthen Athletic

   c) Pontypridd

2. **During the 1995 Rugby World Cup, who were Alex Evans' two assistants?**

   a) Gareth Jenkins and Kevin Bowring

   b) Mike Ruddock and Dennis John

   c) Lynn Howells and Alan Davies

3. **Who stood as a Plaid Cymru candidate in Llanelli during the 1970 general election?**

   a) Carwyn James

   b) Onllwyn Brace

   c) Clem Thomas

4. **Swansea's 2002–03 coach John Connolly was from which country?**

   a) South Africa

   b) Australia

   c) New Zealand

5. **The Barbarians beat Wales 31-24 at the Arms Park in 1990. Who was their captain?**

   a) Stuart Barnes

   b) Nick Farr-Jones

   c) Mike Teague

6. **Wales beat Fiji 31-11 at Buckhurst Park, Suva, in 1969. Which back rower contributed three tries to the haul?**

      a) Dennis Hughes

      b) John Taylor

      c) David Morris

7. **Llandovery beat Cardiff 18-20 in the 2007 Welsh Cup Final. Who scored the injury time try that gave them victory?**

      a) Howard Thomas

      b) Endaf Howells

      c) Owain Rowlands

8. **Name the three Welshmen who played in all three Lions tests during the 1989 tour of Australia.**

9. **After winning ten Welsh caps, who moved from Cardiff to Warrington in 1973?**

10. **New Zealand internationals Aaron and Nathan Mauger's uncle was victorious over Wales in both the 1991 and 1999 World cups representing Western Samoa which later became Samoa. Who was he?**

Round 28

1. **Dafydd James made his international debut in 1996, in Wales' 42-3 defeat to Australia. Which club did he play for at the time?**

    a) Pontypridd
    b) Bridgend
    c) Harlequins

2. **Scott Gibbs scored a famous winning try in Wales' 32-31 win over England at Wembley in 1999, but who scored the Dragons' other try?**

    a) Mark Taylor
    b) Peter Rogers
    c) Shane Howarth

3. **Wales lost 45-41 to club side Suntory in June 2001. Which country's club champions were they?**

    a) Fiji
    b) Tonga
    c) Japan

4. **Who won division one east in 2006–07, but were denied promotion to the Premiership because their ground did not meet the necessary criteria?**

    a) Fleur de Lys
    b) Abercynon
    c) Beddau

5. **Who holds the post war record for *the most appearances in a Swansea shirt*?**

    a) Barry Clegg

    b) Richard Moriaty

    c) Phil Llewellyn

6. **Percy Bush became captain of which famous French side in 1910?**

    a) Nantes

    b) Toulouse

    c) Le Havre

7. **Which woman equalled Gareth Llewellyn's 92 cap Wales record in her country's 15-0 loss to France in 2007?**

    a) Louise Rickard

    b) Liza Burgess

    c) Mellissa Berry

8. **Name the three Llanelli players in the Barbarians side which famously beat New Zealand 23-11 in 1973.**

9. **What did Glyn and Dai do in 1934 that David and Harold did in 1937, and Gareth and Glyn did in 1991?**

10. **Wales selected four club outside halves in their starting line up for their encounter with England in 1988. Name them.**

Round 29

1. Eugene Cross Park is home to which side?

    a) Cwm

    b) Bridgend Athletic

    c) Ebbw Vale

2. Roger Bidgood won five Welsh caps between 1992 and 1993. Which club did he play for at the time?

    a) Newport

    b) Pontypool

    c) Cross Keys

3. Who was Rupert Moon's first Welsh club side?

    a) Neath

    b) Pontypridd

    c) Abertillery

4. Who captained Wales to a 28-3 win over Australia in 1975?

    a) Mervyn Davies

    b) Gareth Edwards

    c) Terry Cobner

5. Who won the first-ever Welsh–Scottish league title in the 1999–2000 season?

    a) Swansea

    b) Newport

    c) Cardiff

6. **Jonathan Davies became the first Welsh outside half to score a try on his debut in fifty four years, during his team's 24-15 win over England in April 1985. Who was the previous player to claim this feat?**

      a) Raymond Ralph

      b) Frank Williams

      c) Dai John

7. **France's 16-6 win over Wales in 1958 was Cliff Morgan's 29th and final game for his country. What else was significant about this encounter?**

      a) The only time an international back row has consisted entirely of three Glamorgan Wanderers players

      b) France's first win at the Arms Park

      c) Clem Thomas' first game as captain

8. **Former Maesteg player Trevor Watkins is grandfather to which member of Wales' 2005 Grand Slam winning team?**

9. **Name the three Aberavon players to tour with the 1977 Lions to New Zealand.**

10. **Which Neath player was sent off in Wales' 23-9, 1995 defeat to England for kicking Ben Clarke in the head?**

Round 30

1. **The son of which famous English cricketer played for Cardiff between 1997 and 2000?**

   a) David Gower

   b) Ian Botham

   c) Geoffrey Boycott

2. **Pontypridd's Gareth Wyatt made a try-scoring debut for Wales against Tonga in 1997, but which position did he play at?**

   a) centre

   b) outside half

   c) full back

3. **Former Llanelli outside half Frano Botica represented which country during the 1999 World Cup qualifying matches?**

   a) Romania

   b) Poland

   c) Croatia

4. **Which African side did Wales beat 15-5 to win the 2006 Hong Kong plate final?**

   a) Namibia

   b) Kenya

   c) Uganda

5. **During the twentieth century only three men captained Swansea in three or more consecutive seasons. The first was Billy Trew between 1906 and 1911. The second was David Richards from 1981 to 1984. Who was the third?**

   a) Mark Davies
   b) Richard Moriaty
   c) Stuart Davies

6. **Richard Parks signed for the Newport Gwent Dragons in the summer of 2007. Which French club did he previously play for?**

   a) Brive
   b) Perpignan
   c) Montpellier

7. **Wales' 14-8 win over Ireland in 1965 included twenty minutes spent by one of the forwards playing full back due to injuries. Who was the forward?**

   a) Alun Pask
   b) Haydn Morgan
   c) Brian Price

8. **Barry John and Gareth Edwards set a Welsh record of 16 appearances together as half backs against Ireland in 1970. Whose record did they beat?**

9. **Who captained the 1977 Lions in New Zealand?**

10. **In 1986, who became the first black player to represent Wales?**

Round 31

1. **J. P. R. Williams played for two different clubs in his time representing Wales. Who were they?**

   a) London Welsh and Bridgend

   b) Cardiff and Richmond

   c) Ebbw Vale and Bristol

2. **The Pacific Islands team that lost 38-29 to Wales in Gareth Jenkins' first win as coach were captained by which former Newport second row?**

   a) Simon Raiwalui

   b) Tevita Taumoepeau

   c) Semo Sititi

3. **Which Ospreys prop captained the region to a 24-16 victory over Australia in 2006?**

   a) Duncan Jones

   b) Paul James

   c) Andrew Millward

4. **Roy Bish became which club's first-ever coach in 1965?**

   a) Cardiff

   b) Newport

   c) Aberavon

5. **Paul Thorburn kicked a penalty goal against Scotland in 1986 which was over 70 yards in distance. The kick was awarded due to a late tackle on Jonathan Davies. Who made the tackle?**

    a) John Jeffrey

    b) Matt Duncan

    c) Finlay Calder

6. **There were two Pontypridd players in Wales' 1995 World cup squad. Neil Jenkins was one. Who was the other?**

    a) Paul John

    b) Mark Rowley

    c) Greg Prosser

7. **Alex Codling left Ebbw Vale as coach in 2007, to join which club as forwards coach?**

    a) London Welsh

    b) Worcester

    c) Bristol

8. **Bridgend full back Howell Davies broke the Welsh record for Five Nations Championship points with a haul of 39 points during the 1984 season. Which two players jointly held the previous 38 point record?**

9. **What was Newport legend Arthur Gould's nickname?**

10. **Which flying winger was named 1990 Welsh Player of the Year?**

Round 32

1. **What colour shirts did Wales wear against red-shirted Tonga in 1974?**
   - a) White
   - b) Green
   - c) Yellow

2. **Swansea and Llanelli both beat the Wallabies in 1992. What did Aled Williams do for Swansea, that Colin Stephens also did for Llanelli?**
   - a) Score a try
   - b) Captain the side
   - c) Kick a drop goal

3. **The Ospreys claimed the 2006–07 Celtic League with a 16-24 win over which Scottish team?**
   - a) Border Reivers
   - b) Glasgow
   - c) Edinburgh

4. **Newport hooker Mike Watkins led his country on his debut in Wales' 18-9 win over Ireland in February 1984. Who did he replace as captain?**
   - a) Jeff Squire
   - b) Eddie Butler
   - c) Gareth Davies

5. **Simon Easterby received a call up to the 2005 Lions tour of New Zealand due to an ankle injury sustained by which player?**

    a) Richard Hill
    b) Lawrence Dallaglio
    c) Simon Taylor

6. **Which Swansea forward won the Man of the Match award in his team's 17-12 victory over Pontypridd in the 1995 Welsh Cup Final?**

    a) Stuart Davies
    b) Rob Appleyard
    c) Paul Arnold

7. **In 1997, who broke the Cardiff record of *most club tries scored in total by an individual*, which had previously been held for 42 years by Bleddyn Williams?**

    a) Nigel Walker
    b) Steve Ford
    c) Mike Rayer

8. **Where did Wales play their first-ever home international – a loss to England in 1882?**

9. **What did Richard Moriaty do in 1987 that Ieuan Evans did in 1991, followed by Mike Hall in 1995?**

10. **Who was the Neath full back that made his international debut at the age of 34 in Wales' 12-9 win over Ireland in 1954, and in the process scored three penalty goals?**

Round 33

1. **Gareth, Jonathan and Rhys were all members of Wales' 2007 World cup squad. What surname do they share?**
    - a) James
    - b) Williams
    - c) Thomas

2. **Which trophy did the Welsh Sevens side win at the 2006 Melbourne Commonwealth Games?**
    - a) Plate
    - b) Fork
    - c) Spoon

3. **Who scored a late drop goal to give Wales a lucky 11-10 win over Fiji in November 2005?**
    - a) Ceri Sweeney
    - b) James Hook
    - c) Nicky Robinson

4. **In 1979, who did Bridgend beat 18-12 to win the Welsh Cup Final?**
    - a) Pontypridd
    - b) Cardiff
    - c) Pontypool

5. **Who wore the Cardiff shirt 410 times between 1952 and 1966?**
    - a) Kingsley Jones
    - b) Alan Pridey
    - c) Lloyd Williams

6. **During Llanelli's humiliating 81-3 defeat to New Zealand in 1997, which All Black crossed the line four times?**

   a) Norm Hewitt

   b) Christian Cullen

   c) Jeff Wilson

7. **Glan yr Afon Park is home to which club side?**

   a) Blackwood

   b) Bargoed

   c) Llandaff North

8. **Which former Pontypool scrum half was the inspiring coach of the national side from 1968 to 1974?**

9. **Gerald Davies won his first cap in 1966 and final cap in 1978 against the same country. Which country?**

10. **Llwynypia forward Dick Hellings scored a try in Wales' 13-3 win over England at Kingsholm, Gloucester in January 1900. What made this remarkable?**

Round 34

1. **Barry John played his 25th and final game for his country against France in 1972. Who famously won his first cap as a substitute in the same game with only two minutes of injury time remaining?**

   a) Derek Quinnell

   b) Roy Bergiers

   c) Jim Shanklin

2. **Who scored 22 points in Wales' 27-18 defeat of England in March 2007?**

   a) Stephen Jones

   b) James Hook

   c) Gavin Henson

3. **Justin Marshall missed the final two league games in the Ospreys 2006–07 title winning season. What was the reason?**

   a) He played for the Classic All Blacks in friendly matches in Japan

   b) He played for the Barbarians in centenary celebration games against Leicester and Bath

   c) He flew back to New Zealand for his brother's wedding

4. **Who scored all of Pontypridd's points in their 20-17 win over Llanelli in the 2002 Welsh Cup Final?**

   a) Brett Davey

   b) Ceri Sweeney

   c) Gareth Wyatt

5. **Mervyn Davies' 37th consecutive game for his country in 1976 made him the most capped Welsh forward. Whose record did he break?**

    a) David Morris
    b) Delme Thomas
    c) Denzil Williams

6. **Who became the first person since Gwyn Nicholls in 1901 to captain Cardiff in three consecutive seasons between 1976 and 1979?**

    a) Mervyn John
    b) Gerald Davies
    c) Barry Nelmes

7. **During Wales' 46-0 win over the United States in 1987, who became the first Welsh substitute to score two tries in a match?**

    a) Anthony Clement
    b) Mike Hall
    c) John Devereux

8. **How many times did Wales record a Grand Slam in the 1970's?**

9. **Who did Llanelli beat 22-3 in a 1999–2000 all Welsh Heineken Cup quarter final?**

10. **Who scored Newport's only try in their 13-8 win over Neath in the 2001 Welsh Cup Final?**

Round 35

1. **Len and Roger Blyth became the eighth father and son combination to play for Wales. Len played in 1951 and 1952, and Roger played between 1974 and 1980. Which club did they both represent?**
   a) Swansea
   b) Bridgend
   c) Aberavon

2. **Who appeared with Gary Olsen and Samantha Janus in the 1998 film *Up and Under*?**
   a) David Bishop
   b) Ray Gravell
   c) Rupert Moon

3. **Who became the first Pontypridd player to win an international cap in 12 years when he came on as a replacement in Wales' 54-9 defeat to New Zealand in 1988?**
   a) Paul Knight
   b) Jonathan Mason
   c) Richie Collins

4. **Tongan international Hale T-Pole signed for the Ospreys in 2007 from which Super 14 side?**
   a) The Highlanders
   b) Western Force
   c) The Sharks

5. **Against which of the following teams have Wales not played an international match?**

   a) New Zealand Army
   b) New Zealand Navy
   c) New Zealand Natives

6. **In 1947, William Gore became which club's first international?**

   a) Newbridge
   b) Maesteg
   c) Treherbert

7. **Who scored the only try of the game on his debut in Wales' 6-0 victory over Scotland in 1974?**

   a) Geoff Wheel
   b) Allan Martin
   c) Terry Cobner

8. **Who scored two drop goals for Bridgend in his team's 16-10 loss to Neath in the 1990 Welsh Cup Final?**

9. **What was the nickname of former Welsh player and manager Clive Rowlands?**

10. **Who was the only member of the Welsh 1999 Rugby World Cup squad to make his debut in the tournament?**

Round 36

1. **What does the J stand for in Welsh legend J. P. R. Williams' name?**
   a) James
   b) Jeremy
   c) John

2. **Who was made Wales head coach for a single international against South Africa in 2007 following the sacking of Gareth Jenkins?**
   a) Neil Jenkins
   b) Rowland Phillips
   c) Nigel Davies

3. **Which Cardiff player made a substitute's appearance against Ireland in 1976, becoming only the 16th player used during the Grand Slam winning campaign?**
   a) Mike Knill
   b) Brynmor Williams
   c) Gareth Davies

4. **In 1989, who became Wales' 100th captain in a full international in Scotland's 23-7 win?**
   a) Kevin Phillips
   b) Robert Jones
   c) Paul Thorburn

5. **Who beat Swansea by a goal to nil, to win the first-ever South Wales Challenge Cup in the 1877–78 season?**

   a) Newport

   b) Llandaff

   c) Pontymister

6. **Penygraig RFC had 19 players, each given an 18 month ban from rugby in 2003. What was their crime?**

   a) Missing a drugs test after the silver ball Cup Final against Pontypridd

   b) Being involved in a 34 man brawl during their Welsh cup match against Ynysybwl

   c) Caught in a betting scam where money was put on them to lose against Ystrad Rhondda

7. **Fiji bravely lost to Wales 28-22 at Cardiff Arms Park in 1964. Who was the Fijian prop that scored a hat-trick of touch downs?**

   a) Sela Toga

   b) Sevaro Walisoliso

   c) Aporosa Robe

8. **Who made a substitute appearance for Wales with only 20 minutes left on the clock against England in 1970, turning the match around from being 6-13 down, to winning 17-13?**

9. **Why did referee Jack Taylor order the whole Welsh team off the field, half way through the second half of their 1957 game against Ireland?**

10. **Who scored 27 tries, 222 conversions and 281 penalties in 273 games for Pontypridd during the 1970s?**

Round 37

1. Robert Howley won 59 Welsh caps between 1996 and 2002. What position did he play?

    a) prop

    b) scrum half

    c) full back

2. Which ground, home of Ulster saw Wales beat Ireland 15-3 in 1931?

    a) Ravenhill

    b) Blackbird Rock

    c) Crowfield

3. Who scored a brace of tries on his 50th international in Wales' 72-18 defeat of Japan in 2007?

    a) Kevin Morgan

    b) Dafydd James

    c) Shane Williams

4. Newport beat which side 16-15 to win their first Welsh cup in 1977?

    a) Bridgend

    b) Cardiff

    c) Swansea

5. Who won the accolade of Man of the Match in Wales' 47–8 victory over Italy in 2008?

    a) Shane Williams

    b) Stephen Jones

    c) Lee Byrne

6. **Swansea legend Billy Trew refused to play for Wales against Ireland in 1907. What was his reason?**

   a) He felt his team mate Fred Scrine had been harshly treated by being suspended for using improper language to a referee

   b) The WRU had booked the committee and their wives into a four star Dublin hotel while the players had to stay in a bed and breakfast

   c) Fellow Swansea player Frank Gordon had again been overlooked for a cap, which Trew believed was due to a bias towards Cardiff players

7. **During Wales' 15-12 defeat of Scotland in 1992, who became the last Welshman to score a 4 point try?**

   a) Emyr Lewis

   b) Stuart Davies

   c) Richard Webster

8. **In 1998, who won his 15th and final Welsh cap, eight years after winning his 14th cap?**

9. **During Wales' 1976 Grand Slam winning Five Nations campaign, who were the two wingers used?**

10. **Which Pontypool second row made his Wales debut in the 1982, 22-12 win over France?**

Round 38

1. **Black and Amber are the traditional colours of which club side?**
   - a) Cardiff
   - b) Glamorgan Wanderers
   - c) Newport

2. **Which prop won 51 caps for Wales between 1987 and 2001?**
   - a) Mike Griffiths
   - b) Spencer John
   - c) David Young

3. **If you subtracted the total number of points that Gareth Edwards scored for Wales from the total that Iestyn Harris scored, what would be the answer?**
   - a) 20
   - b) 40
   - c) 80

4. **Which rugby player was BBC Wales Sports Personality of the Year in 1997?**
   - a) Ieuan Evans
   - b) Scott Gibbs
   - c) Scott Quinnell

5. **Who became the third Welshman to score a hat-trick of tries on his debut, during his country's 49-11 victory over Zimbabwe in 1998?**

      a) John Funnell

      b) Richard Rees

      c) Byron Hayward

6. **David Jones between 1902 and 1906, and Stan Davies in 1923, are the only two internationals from which club side?**

      a) Treherbert

      b) Penarth

      c) Brynmawr

7. **Jeff Squire became the first Welsh captain of the 1980s, but who was the second?**

      a) Steve Fenwick

      b) Gareth Davies

      c) Terry Holmes

8. **Which second row holds the record for the most appearances for Llanelli?**

9. **Which former full back is the only Welsh international to have been born on mainland Europe?**

10. **These players all carried out the same feat: James Bevan in 1881, Charles Lewis in 1882, John Evans in 1934, Clive Rowlands in 1963 and Mike Watkins in 1984. What was the feat?**

Round 39

1. **Who was made Wales head coach on December 1st 2007?**

   a) Robbie Deans
   b) Matt Williams
   c) Warren Gatland

2. **Welsh internationals Vernon and Gareth share which surname?**

   a) Cooper
   b) Builder
   c) Plumber

3. **Neil Jenkins played one season in 2003-2004 for which side?**

   a) Bath
   b) Celtic Warriors
   c) Bedwas

4. **With three tries to his name, who was Wales' top try scorer during the 1976 Grand Slam winning campaign?**

   a) J. P. R. Williams
   b) Gareth Edwards
   c) Gerald Davies

5. **Scotland's George Lindsey set a record against Wales in 1887 which has never been beaten. What was it?**

   a) He scored five tries, the most scored in a Five Nations match
   b) He scored a try after 38 seconds, the fastest try in Five Nations history
   c) He kicked a Five Nations record of eight conversions in a game

6. **Which Cardiff legend achieved the feat of being an Oxford Blue at rugby and boxing, as well as Berkshire county half mile champion, and to top it off, carried the flame in the 1948 London Olympics?**

      a) Jack Matthews

      b) Haydn Tanner

      c) C. Derek Williams

7. **Eleven-times-capped prop John Robins was appointed to which position in 1966?**

      a) First Lions coach

      b) First secretary of the Welsh Rugby Union

      c) First-ever coach of Leicester

8. **In Wales' first-ever victory over South Africa in 1999, who was the only Newport player in the Welsh side?**

9. **Name the three men to have captained Wales in both rugby codes.**

10. **Aberavon's George Vickery became an international in 1905. His son Walter, who also played for Aberavon, became an international in 1938. What was unusual about these distinctions?**

Round 40

1. **Which Boobyer brother received a full Welsh cap?**

    a) Neil

    b) Ian

    c) Roddy

2. **How many tries did Nigel Walker score for Wales?**

    a) 12

    b) 22

    c) 32

3. **Against Romania in 2001, who became the 10th Welshman to earn 50 caps?**

    a) Colin Charvis

    b) Robert Howley

    c) Garin Jenkins

4. **This 19-times-capped second row, packed down with Gareth Llewellyn, Greg Prosser, Paul Arnold and Andy Moore during his 1990s international career. Who is he?**

    a) Anthony Copsey

    b) Derwyn Jones

    c) Stuart Roy

5. **Wales beat Scotland 25-21 at Murrayfield in 1985. Who scored both tries for the away side?**

    a) Terry Holmes

    b) Mark Titley

    c) David Pickering

6. **Which hotel became the spiritual home for the Barbarians, where they would stay on their Easter tours of Wales?**

   a) Angel Hotel, Cardiff

   b) Esplanade Hotel, Penarth

   c) Beaumont Hotel, Swansea

7. **Who was named scrum half in Wales' first game following Gareth Edward's retirement in 1978?**

   a) Terry Holmes

   b) Brynmor Williams

   c) Gerald Williams

8. **Who were the two Pontypridd players in the Welsh side that famously beat France 34-33 in 1999?**

9. **Who won the first of his 32 caps against Ireland in 1974 and the last against the same opposition in 1982?**

10. **John Parfitt against England in 1894 became the first person to do it, while Barry John became the last to do it, against France in 1971. Nobody will ever do this again. What was it?**

Round 41

1. **Ynysybwl-born Garin Jenkins won 59 Welsh caps. What was his recognised position?**

   a) Number 8

   b) Hooker

   c) Second row

2. **Which prop successfully sued Olivier Merle for causing him an ankle injury in 1995, where video evidence was used in a French court for the first time?**

   a) Laurence Delaney

   b) Ricky Evans

   c) Christian Loader

3. **Which Italian received a four-week ban following his punch on Stephen Jones in Italy's 2007 six nations win over Wales?**

   a) Mauro Bergamasco

   b) Gonzalo Canale

   c) Kaine Robertson

4. **Who played scrum half in Wales' 24-15 win over England at Twickenham in 1984?**

   a) Terry Holmes

   b) David Bishop

   c) Robert Jones

5. **In 2004, which 28-times-capped Welsh forward became Coventry head coach?**

   a) Kingsley Jones
   b) Steve Williams
   c) Richard Webster

6. **During Swansea's 1991-92 league winning season, who was their top try scorer?**

   a) Mark Titley
   b) David Weatherley
   c) Simon Davies

7. **If Edward Treharne was the first, and Tom Williams was the second, then who was the third Pontypridd player to represent Wales?**

   a) Glyn Davies
   b) Ernest George
   c) Russell Robins

8. **How many Ospreys players took to the field in Wales' 19-26 victory over England in 2008?**

9. **Who did Wales lose to in the 1987 Rugby World Cup semi final?**

10. **Glyn John made his Welsh rugby union debut against England in 1954 even though he had already played rugby league for Leigh. How was this allowed?**

Round 42

1. **Paul Turner became coach of which side in 2005?**

   a) Newport Gwent Dragons

   b) Crumlin

   c) Sale Sharks

2. **Which of the following is able to say that they captained their country on home soil at three different venues, the Arms Park, Wembley and Millenium Stadium?**

   a) Colin Charvis

   b) Gareth Thomas

   c) Jonathan Humphreys

3. **Full back Lee Byrne began his career at which club?**

   a) Bridgend Athletic

   b) Tondu

   c) Bridgend

4. **Dual code rugby player Danny Wilson is father to which football player?**

   a) Ryan Giggs

   b) Craig Bellamy

   c) Robert Earnshaw

5. **Mike Rayer scored two tries against Scotland in 1994 after coming off the bench. Which of his Cardiff club mates did he replace?**

   a) Mike Hall

   b) Simon Hill

   c) Nigel Walker

6. **Who made his 100th Llanelli Scarlets appearance, against Border Reivers in 2007?**

   a) Simon Easterby
   b) John Davies
   c) Dafydd Jones

7. **Which of the following amassed 400 appearances for Pontypridd during the 1960s and 1970s?**

   a) Arfon Jones
   b) Gareth Thomas
   c) Alyn Paul

8. **Barry John retired from rugby at the age of 27 in 1972. Which other famous outside half did the same in 1958?**

9. **Name the two full backs used by Wales during the 1986 season.**

10. **What links Welsh internationals Max Wiltshire, Gwilym Wilkins and Jason Jones-Hughes?**

Round 43

1. **Singer Charlotte Church had a baby in 2007 with which Welsh international rugby player?**
   a) James Hook
   b) Jamie Robinson
   c) Gavin Henson

2. **Former Cardiff flanker Dan Baugh won 27 caps for which country?**
   a) Canada
   b) Australia
   c) Scotland

3. **Ynysangharad fields were home to which club side between 1908 and 1974?**
   a) Pontypridd
   b) Cross Keys
   c) Maesteg

4. **Which English test cricketer played rugby for both Aberavon and Newport?**
   a) Graham Gooch
   b) Hugh Morris
   c) Matthew Maynard

5. **During the 1970s, who made the most capped appearances for Wales?**
   a) Gareth Edwards
   b) Gerald Davies
   c) J. P. R. Williams

6. **Wales beat Scotland 23-10 in February 2004. In that game, who became the first Welshman to win a cap while representing a French club?**

   a) Gareth Llewellyn
   b) Stephen Jones
   c) Colin Charvis

7. **Johnny Williams scored 17 tries in 17 internationals between 1906 and 1911. Who did one better by scoring 17 tries in just 16 internationals during the same period?**

   a) Reggie Gibbs
   b) Rhys Gabe
   c) Billy Trew

8. **Glen Webbe was forced to return home early from the 1987 Rugby World Cup with concussion. Which Swansea winger replaced him in the squad?**

9. **Which four-times-capped international scored a club record 39 points for Llanelli against Newport on the 19th of September 1992?**

10. **Who formed the second row partnership in Wales' 1978 Grand Slam winning campaign?**

Round 44

1. **Alfie is the well-known nickname of which Welsh international?**
   - a) Gareth Thomas
   - b) Rhys Williams
   - c) Kevin Morgan

2. **Neath's Chris Bridges won seven caps in the early 1990s. Which position did he play?**
   - a) Scrum half
   - b) Centre
   - c) Wing

3. **Which of the following clubs would you not expect to see wearing black and blue?**
   - a) Llanharan
   - b) Cardiff
   - c) Maesteg

4. **Fiji international Nicky Little made 14 appearances for which side during the 2001–02 season?**
   - a) Caerphilly
   - b) Newport
   - c) Pontypridd

5. **Who scored Wales' only try in their 12-9 win over England in 1989?**
   - a) Mike Griffiths
   - b) Paul Turner
   - c) Mike Hall

6. **Norman Gale's appearance against New Zealand in 1967 was marked by an unusual feat. What was it?**

   a) He stayed on the pitch for the whole game even though he broke his arm in the fifth minute

   b) He became the only hooker to score a penalty in a Welsh jersey

   c) He crossed the try line twice but both times the try was disallowed

7. **Louise Rickard won her 90th cap in Wales' 10-5 win over Ireland in 2007. Which London club did she represent?**

   a) Wasps

   b) Saracens

   c) London Welsh

8. **For which two clubs did Barry John play for?**

9. **At which ground did Wales play their first-ever World Cup match?**

10. **On 2 May 1998, who were the father and son combination that appeared together for Swansea in their 71-19 victory over Bridgend?**

Round 45

1. **Who scored 216 points in 23 internationals between 1995 and 2001?**

   a) Lee Jarvis

   b) Arwel Thomas

   c) Craig Warlow

2. **Graeme Maw was unveiled on 3 January 2008 as WRU elite performance director. What previous job did he have?**

   a) Performance director for the British triathlon association

   b) Head coach of Bedford RFC

   c) Bodyguard to Prince Charles

3. **Who scored 80 tries in 119 appearances for Pontypridd during the 1990s?**

   a) Kevin Morgan

   b) Geraint O. Lewis

   c) David Manley

4. **Abertillery scrum half Allan Lewis played six times for his country during the 1960s. Which of the following outside halves did he not play with?**

   a) Barry John

   b) David Watkins

   c) Phil Bennet

5. **Who holds the record for the Welshman with the most appearances, 23 in all, for the Barbarians?**
   a) Rhys 'R. H.' Williams
   b) Tommy David
   c) Phil Bennet

6. **Who captained Llanelli to a 23-9 win over Newport in the 2003 Welsh Cup Final?**
   a) Scott Quinnell
   b) Leigh Davies
   c) Robin McBryde

7. **Ryan Jones played junior football as a goalkeeper for which club side?**
   a) Swansea City
   b) Bristol City
   c) Reading

8. **Argentina played Samoa in the 1999 rugby World Cup at which Welsh ground?**

9. **Which Ynysybwl born prop forward won ten Welsh caps and three British Lions caps in the 1980's?**

10. **On 7 April 1984, why was there an anti-apartheid demonstration on the streets of Cardiff?**

Round 46

1. **Who was the English referee that controversially whistled for full-time at the end of Wales' 23-20 loss to Italy in 2007, even though he'd previously suggested that there would be enough time for one final line-out?**

   a) Chris White

   b) Dave Pearson

   c) Tony Spreadbury

2. **Outside half legend Jonathan Davies did not play for which of the following clubs?**

   a) Neath

   b) Cross Keys

   c) Cardiff

3. **With three tries to his credit, who was Wales' top try scorer during the 1997 Five Nations tournament?**

   a) Robert Howley

   b) Scott Quinnell

   c) Ieuan Evans

4. **Whose drop goal won the 2006 Welsh Cup Final for Pontypridd against Neath?**

   a) Dai Flanagan

   b) Morgan Stoddart

   c) Gareth Jones

5. **John Dawes selected a centre on the wing in Wales' 13-12 win over Romania in 1979. Who was he?**

    a) Roy Bergiers

    b) Steve Fenwick

    c) Ray Gravell

6. **Which of the following scored the most points for Wales?**

    a) Jack Bancroft

    b) Gareth Edwards

    c) Barry John

7. **Moascar, Egypt, is the place of birth of which former prop forward?**

    a) Graham Price

    b) Mike Knill

    c) Boyo James

8. **Name the second row that scored Wales' only try, in their 16-7 defeat of Argentina in the 1991 Rugby World Cup.**

9. **On the 23rd February 1909, Wales played their first match in which European country?**

10. **What was exceptional about Watcyn Thomas' appearance for Wales against Scotland in 1931?**

Round 47

1. **Against Scotland in 2001, who became the first Welshman to record three drop goals in a match?**
    a) Stephen Jones
    b) Arwel Thomas
    c) Neil Jenkins

2. **Where was the 1999 Welsh Cup Final, a 37-10 win for Swansea over Llanelli held?**
    a) Old Trafford
    b) Ninian Park
    c) The Vetch

3. **Who scored 20 tries in 46 Internationals between 1966 and 1978?**
    a) Gerald Davies
    b) John Dawes
    c) J. J. Williams

4. **Who directly preceded Robert Howley as Welsh captain?**
    a) Paul John
    b) Gwyn Jones
    c) Jonathan Humphreys

5. **Shaun Edwards was named Wales' part-time defence coach in January 2008. Which of the following rugby league sides did he not play for?**

      a) London Broncos

      b) St Helen's

      c) Bradford Bulls

6. **Mark de Marigny, brother of Italy outside half Roland, signed for which Premiership club in 2006?**

      a) Ebbw Vale

      b) Llandovery

      c) Cardiff

7. **New Zealand full back Fergus McCormick set a world record for *points scored in a match* against Wales at Eden Park in 1969. How many points did he score?**

      a) 18

      b) 21

      c) 24

8. **Who scored the first try in the new Millenium stadium, in a game against South Africa in 1999?**

9. **In 1968, who became the first Welshman to win a British Lions cap as a replacement, and repeated the feat during the 1971 tour?**

10. **Name the four outside halves that Gareth Edwards played with during his 53 internationals.**

Round 48

1. **Back row forward Emyr Lewis played for which two clubs during the 1990s?**

   a) Swansea and Pontypool

   b) Llanelli and Cardiff

   c) Neath and Tondu

2. **Which French side famously beat Pontypridd 25-20 in the 1997–98 Heineken cup quarter final play off?**

   a) Pau

   b) Bourgoin

   c) Brive

3. **Wales' 1994 Five Nations championship winning pack contained one Swansea player. Who was he?**

   a) Garin Jenkins

   b) Paul Arnold

   c) Ian Buckett

4. **Colin Charvis' 21st international try, scored against Canada in 2007 equalled the record of tries scored by a forward. Whose record did it equal?**

   a) Neil Back

   b) Carlo Checchinato

   c) Michael Jones

5. **During Wales' 16-7 Grand Slam clinching result over France in 1978, who scored both of the home team's tries?**

   a) Steve Fenwick

   b) J. J. Williams

   c) Phil Bennett

6. **Alban Davies captained Wales in 1914. What was his role outside rugby?**

   a) Clergyman

   b) Policeman

   c) Taxidermist

7. **Who scored 37 points in 24 internationals between 1983 and 1989?**

   a) Malcolm Dacey

   b) Adrian Hadley

   c) Bleddyn Bowen

8. **Who coached the 1977 British Lions on their tour of New Zealand?**

9. **What did Willie Llewellyn do against England in 1899, that Reggie Gibbs did against France in 1908 and Ieuan Evans did against Canada in 1987?**

10. **The Barbarians 23-11 victory over New Zealand in 1973 will always be remembered for Gareth Edward's famous try, but which other two Welshmen also crossed the whitewash on that occasion?**

Round 49

1. **Which Tumble-born scrum half won 3 British Lions caps on their 2005 tour of New Zealand?**
   - a) Dwayne Peel
   - b) Gareth Cooper
   - c) Mike Phillips

2. **With 32 in total, who holds the record for most appearances at the National Stadium, Cardiff Arms Park?**
   - a) Robert Jones
   - b) Ieuan Evans
   - c) Gareth Llewellyn

3. **What's the connection between Geoff Lewis' appearance against England in 1960 and Craig Quinnell's appearance against the same country in 1999?**
   - a) Both played for Richmond
   - b) Both had an older brother who'd already played for Wales
   - c) They were both late call-ups on the day of the game due to injuries to others, but managed to score a try each

4. **Arthur Lewis in 1973 became the first person from which club to captain Wales?**
   - a) Pontypool
   - b) Ebbw Vale
   - c) Abertillery

5. **Who holds Swansea's post-war club record of most career points?**

    a) Roger Blyth

    b) Arwel Thomas

    c) Mark Wyatt

6. **26-times-capped England scrum half Dewi Morris was born in which Welsh town?**

    a) Crickhowell

    b) Aberystwyth

    c) Penarth

7. **Who scored the two tries in Wales' 13-8 victory over New Zealand in 1953?**

    a) Gerwyn Williams and Gwyn Rowlands

    b) Cliff Morgan and Bleddyn Williams

    c) Sid Judd and Ken Jones

8. **Old Deer Park is home to which club side?**

9. **Aberavon beat which European country 42-0 in the 1998–99 WRU challenge cup?**

10. **Which former Great Britain rugby league international scored three tries in five games for Pontypridd during a short spell in South Wales in the 2000–01 season?**

Round 50

1. **Michael Owen decided to leave the Newport Gwent Dragons in 2008 to join which English side?**

   a) Wasps

   b) Newcastle

   c) Saracens

2. **Internationals Mike, Rowland and Kevin share which surname?**

   a) Philips

   b) Rees

   c) Lewis

3. **Which of the following forwards did not win a European challenge cup medal in the 2005–06 season when Gloucester beat London Irish 36-34?**

   a) Mefin Davies

   b) Gareth Delve

   c) Gary Powell

4. **Miss Wales 2003 Imogen Thomas was a contestant on reality television programme *Big Brother* 7. Which former Llanelli forward is her father?**

   a) Delme Thomas

   b) Charlie Thomas

   c) Carwyn Thomas

5. Which team lost to Cardiff in the final of both the 1981 and 1982 Welsh cup?

      a) Bridgend

      b) Aberavon

      c) Swansea

6. Who was manager of the 1974 British and Irish Lions tour of South Africa?

      a) John Dawes

      b) Clive Rowlands

      c) Alun Thomas

7. Who kicked two penalties in order to give Wales a 6-0 victory over Australia in 1947?

      a) Bill Tamplin

      b) Frank Trott

      c) Lewis Jones

8. Who became Elite Performance Director for the Ospreys in 2007?

9. What was the name of the South Wales rugby league side which union internationals Brynmor Williams, Steve Fenwick and Tom David all played for?

10. Who was Wales head coach for 14 matches between 1980 and 1982?

Answers

Round 1

1. a
2. a
3. b
4. b
5. b
6. c
7. a
8. Due to a fixture mix up, both games had to be played on the same day – one before, and the other after lunch.
9. Garin Jenkins. The only back row player on the bench was Martyn Morris who had already been used to replace Phil May.
10. This was the first match played under floodlights at Sardis Road.

Round 2

1. a
2. b
3. a
4. b. Wales beat Japan 57-10 during the '95 World Cup.
5. c
6. b
7. c
8. There were allegations of professionalism in the Welsh game.
9. Penclawdd
10. Paul Thorburn, Paul Moriaty and Adrian Hadley.

Round 3

1. c
2. c
3. a
4. c
5. c
6. a
7. c. Swansea won 11-3.
8. Brynmor Williams
9. Ray Williams
10. Bryn Terfel, Aled Jones and Katherine Jenkins.

Round 4

1. a
2. a
3. c
4. c
5. b
6. b
7. c. Newport won 11-0.
8. First-ever points scored by the Ospreys in a competitive match. Ospreys beat Ulster 41-30.
9. David Nash against South Africa in 1960.
10. Dewi Bebb

Round 5

1. a
2. b
3. b
4. c
5. b. 7 players.
6. a

7. c
8. Reg Skrimshire
9. Maurice Richards
10. Bleddyn Taylor

Round 6

1. b
2. b. Against England.
3. c. Paul John took over when Chris Wyatt replaced Kingsley Jones, Garin Jenkins became captain when Dai Llewellyn took the field instead of Paul John.
4. a
5. b
6. c. Kicked the ball dead.
7. b
8. Ian Stephens (Bridgend) 1 cap, Staff Jones (Pontypool) 3 caps.
9. Bath. London Welsh lost 24-15.
10. The WRU contributed to a testimonial fund which was considered a degree of professionalism.

Round 7

1. c
2. b. At the World Youth Festival.
3. a. Wales won 40-9.
4. b
5. b
6. c. Wales won by 2 goals, 2 tries to nil at Lansdowne Road.
7. b
8. Zimbabwe (17 caps, 4 tries) and South Africa (28 caps, 4 tries).
9. Tom Shanklin (son of Jim), Craig Quinnell

(son of Derek) and Jamie Ringer (son of Paul).

10. Diana, Princess of Wales.

Round 8

1. b. Losing to Sale 22-25 at the Kassam stadium, Oxford.

2. c

3. c

4. b. Winning 18-6 away in the 1998–99 European shield.

5. c

6. a

7. b

8. Kicking directly to touch outside the 22 meter line. This was a tactic used by Clive Rowlands against Scotland at Murrayfield in 1963, resulting in 111 line-outs.

9. First-ever Osprey to receive a yellow card.

10 Jason Forster.

Round 9

1. b

2. c. Graham Price, Charlie Faulkner and Bobby Windsor.

3. b. Newport 1977 and Pontypool 1983.

4. b

5. b

6. a

7. c

8. Matt Pini

9. 4 x 100 yards relay, at the 1948 Olynpics in London.

10. They all captained Wales against England on their

international debuts. Clive Rowlands in 1963, John R Evans in 1934 and James Bevan in 1881.

Round 10

1. b
2. c. Michael Lynagh's total was 911 points.
3. c
4. c
5. a. A try and two penalties.
6. c. Gareth Evans played in 3 tests.
7. a
8. Grannygate, the story suggesting that Shane Howarth and Brett Sinkinson had no Welsh parentage.
9. Jonathan Davies, John Deveraux and Paul Moriaty.
10. Cardiff College of Education.

Round 11

1. b
2. a
3. b
4. a. They only played in the 2003–04 competition, winning 4 out of 6 games.
5. c
6. a
7. c. They lost 24-15.
8. Viv Jenkins
9. Llandovery College
10. Derek Quinell, Mervyn Davies and John Taylor.

Round 12

1. a
2. c

3. a. Twice for Cardiff in 1973 and 1977.
4. c
5. a. Dafydd Jones, Dwayne Peel and Mark Taylor for Wales, Simon Easterby for Ireland.
6. c
7. a
8. Jack Morley
9. Newbridge
10. Scored a try on their Lions debut.

Round 13

1. a
2. a
3. c
4. b
5. c
6. a
7. b
8. Robert Howley
9. Bob Penberthy
10. Gwyn Nicholls

Round 14

1. a. One draw from three games.
2. c
3. a
4. b
5. a
6. c
7. b. Previously Wales would field two full backs.
8. Tommy Harris. No other hooker had ever played in more Great Britain tests previously.

9. Peter Rogers, having played for all three sides amongst others.
10. Rod Snow

Round 15

1. c
2. c
3. b
4. a
5. b. 22-32 at the Brewery Field.
6. b. Previously only three three-quarters were used and nine forwards.
7. a
8. Ryan Jones
9. Sean and Rory Lamont
10. Allan Martin

Round 16

1. a
2. b
3. c
4. a
5. b
6. b
7. a
8. Bryn Meredith
9. Cronulla Sharks
10. Ivor Jones

Round 17

1. b
2. a
3. b
4. c
5. c. In a Cardiff v South Wales Police game.
6. a
7. b
8. Carwyn James
9. Jonathan Davies
10. 48th and final Aberavon player to be capped by Wales.

Round 18

1. a
2. c
3. a. Resigned after four games.
4. a
5. c
6. b
7. c
8. Bleddyn Williams
9. They had to borrow two Welsh players as a couple of theirs didn't turn up. Wales won.
10. Lee Byrne and Mike Phillips.

Round 19

1. c
2. c
3. b
4. a. In 1989, 1997 and 2001.
5. a

6. b
7. a
8. Stuart Davies
9. St David's College, Lampeter.
10. Sid Going

Round 20

1. a. He received a four-week suspension and £5,000 fine for aggressively attempting to enter seating area and making an offensive hand gesture.
2. b
3. c
4. a
5. c
6. b. He also scored the only Welsh try.
7. c
8. Resolven
9. Billy James
10. Colin Smart

Round 21

1. a
2. a
3. b
4. b
5. a
6. c
7. a
8. John Dawes in 1971 to Australia and New Zealand.
9. Kevin Moseley
10. Edinburgh Wanderers

Round 22

1. c
2. b
3. a
4. c. 154 tries in 209 games
5. c. Glen Webbe, Mike Hall, John Devereux and Richard Diplock.
6. b
7. c
8. Ceri Sweeney
9. Phil May, who went on to earn a total of seven caps.
10. Neil Jenkins

Round 23

1. b
2. c
3. c. Following a mass brawl on the pitch.
4. a
5. a
6. b
7. c
8. Pieter Muller
9. Paul Emmerick
10. Norman Gale (Llanelli) who replaced Jeff Young (Bridgend).

Round 24

1. c. Losing 40-12 to Castres
2. b. In 2004
3. a
4. c
5. b

6. a. Geoff Whitson, Glyn Davidge and Brian Cresswell.
7. a. Wales won 6-0.
8. Barry John
9. Derek Bevan
10. Robert Ackerman

Round 25

1. a
2. c
3. b
4. c
5. c
6. a
7. c
8. Paul Jones
9. Wales lost 16-13 to Western Samoa.
10. Leeds Rugby League

Round 26

1. c
2. a. The previous Englishman to score four tries in a match was Neil Back against the Netherlands.
3. b
4. a
5. b
6. c
7. c
8. Hemi Taylor, making his debut in Wales' 102-11 win over Portugal in 1994.
9. Elgan Rees
10. This was due to Swansea and Cardiff's decision to play English clubs during their rebel season.

Round 27

1. c
2. b
3. a
4. b
5. b
6. a. Although John Taylor did score twice.
7. b
8. Ieuan Evans, Robert Jones and David Young.
9. John Bevan
10. Stephen Bachop, he also played in five tests for New Zealand.

Round 28

1. b
2. c
3. c
4. c
5. b. 472 appearances, 32 tries.
6. a
7. a
8. Phil Bennett, Tommy David and Derek Quinnell.
9. They were all brother that played together for Neath and Wales- Glyn and Dai Prosser, David and Harold Thomas, Gareth and Glyn Llewellyn.
10. Jonathan Davies(Llanelli), Bleddyn Bowen(South Wales Police), Mark Ring(Pontypool) and Anthony Clement(Swansea).

Round 29

1. c
2. a

3. c
4. a
5. c
6. a. In a 35-3 win over France in 1931.
7. b
8. Gavin Henson
9. Allan Martin, Clive Williams and John Bevan.
10. John Davies

Round 30

1. b. Liam Botham
2. c
3. c. Due to a Croatian grandmother.
4. b
5. b
6. b
7. a
8. Dick Jones and Dicky Owen, both from Swansea played fifteen times together between 1901 and 1910.
9. Phil Bennett
10. Glen Webbe

Round 31

1. a
2. a
3. b
4. a
5. c
6. c
7. a
8. Phil Bennett(1976) and Steve Fenwick(1979).

9. Monkey
10. Arthur Emyr

Round 32

1. b
2. c. Swansea won 21-6, Llanelli won 13-9.
3. a
4. b
5. b
6. c
7. b. Williams scored 185 tries, Ford scored 198 tries.
8. St Helen's
9. They were Wales' World Cup captains.
10. Viv Evans

Round 33

1. c
2. a
3. c
4. a
5. b
6. b
7. a
8. Clive Rowlands
9. Australia
10. He played almost the whole game with a fractured forearm.

Round 34

1. a
2. b
3. a

4. a
5. c
6. b
7. a
8. Three times: 1971, 1976 and 1978.
9. Cardiff
10. Adrian Garvey

Round 35

1. a
2. b
3. b
4. a
5. b
6. a
7. c .
8. Aled Williams
9. Top Cat
10. Jason Jones-Hughes, in Wales' 23-18 victory over Argentina as a substitute for Scott Gibbs.

Round 36

1. c
2. c
3. a
4. c
5. a
6. a
7. b
8. Ray 'Chicko' Hopkins
9. To change jerseys because they were covered in mud, Wales went on to win 6-5.
10. Colin Bolderson

Round 37

1. b
2. a
3. c
4. b
5. c
6. a
7. c
8. Mark Jones, he won his final cap against Zimbabwe after returning from rugby league.
9. Gerald Davies and J. J. Williams.
10. Steve Sutton

Round 38

1. c
2. c
3. a. Gareth Edwards scored 88 points, Iestyn Harris scored 108 points.
4. b
5. c
6. a
7. a
8. Phil May, 552 appearances.
9. Paul Thorburn, born in Rheindalen, West Germany.
10. They all captained Wales on their debut.

Round 39

1. c
2. a
3. b
4. b
5. a
6. c
7. a
8. Peter Rogers
9. David Watkins, Jonathan Davies and David Young.
10. George played for England, while Walter played for Wales.

Round 40

1. a
2. a
3. b
4. b
5. c
6. b
7. b
8. Dafydd James and Neil Jenkins.
9. Geoff Wheel
10. Scoring a three point try for Wales.

Round 41

1. b
2. b
3. a
4. a
5. b
6. c

7. b
8. 14 (13 started and Ian Evans came off the bench).
9. New Zealand 49-6.
10. He repaid his £400 signing on fee to Leigh and was reinstated because he had become a professional while still at school at the age of 17.

Round 42

1. a
2. c
3. a
4. a
5. c
6. b
7. a
8. Cliff Morgan
9. Paul Thorburn and Malcolm Dacey.
10. They were all born in Australia.

Round 43

1. c
2. a
3. a
4. b
5. c. 44 appearances in the 1970s.
6. c, Tarbes
7. a
8. Mark Titley
9. Colin Stephens
10. Allan Martin and Geoff Wheel.

Round 44

1. a
2. a
3. c
4. c
5. c
6. b
7. b
8. Llanelli and Cardiff
9. Athletic Park, Wellington, Wales beat Ireland 13-6.
10. Keith and Dean Colclough, Hooker Dean came on with a few minutes to go joining prop Keith on his 431st and final game for the club.

Round 45

1. b
2. a
3. c
4. c
5. a
6. b
7. b
8. Stradey Park, Llanelli
9. Staff Jones
10. In protest to the selection of 3 South African players in a WRU President's World XV, to play Wales in a match to mark the completion of the National Stadium.

Round 46

1. a
2. b

3. c
4. a
5. c
6. c. Jack Bancroft and Gareth Edwards both scored 88 points, Barry John scored 90.
7. a
8. Paul Arnold
9. France, Wales won 47-5
10. He played 70 minutes with a broken collarbone but still scored a try. Wales won 13-8.

Round 47

1. c
2. b
3. a
4. b
5. b
6. b
7. c. three conversions, five penalties and one drop goal, beating the previous record of 22 jointly held by South Africa's Dietlef Mare and England's Douglas Lambert.
8. Mark Taylor
9. Delme Thomas
10. David Watkins, Barry John, Phil Bennett and John Bevan.

Round 48

1. b
2. c
3. a
4. b
5. c

6. a
7. c. Malcolm Dacey scored 36 points in 15 internationals while Adrian Hadley scored 36 points in 27 internationals.
8. John Dawes
9. Score 4 tries in a match.
10. John Bevan and J. P. R. Williams.

Round 49

1. a
2. b
3. a
4. b
5. c. 2740 points(55 tries, 466 penalties, 6 drop goals, 552 conversions).
6. a
7. c
8. London Welsh
9. Georgia
10. Alan Hunte

Round 50

1. c
2. a
3. b
4. b
5. a
6. c
7. a
8. Andrew Hore
9. Blue Dragons
10. John Lloyd

This book is just one of a whole range of publications from Y Lolfa. For a full list of books currently in print, send now for your free copy of our new full-colour catalogue. Or simply surf into our website

www.ylolfa.com

for secure on-line ordering.

TALYBONT CEREDIGION CYMRU SY24 5AP
e-mail ylolfa@ylolfa.com
website www.ylolfa.com
phone (01970) 832 304
fax 832 782